Mr. Happy Heart

by Marci M. White

To my daughter, Amber - the happiest heart I know.

Order this book online at www.trafford.com
or email orders@trafford.com

Most Trafford titles are also available at major online book retailers.

 www.trafford.com

North America & international
toll-free: 844 688 6899 (USA & Canada)
fax: 812 355 4082

Our mission is to efficiently provide the world's finest, most comprehensive book publishing service, enabling every author to experience success. To find out how to publish your book, your way, and have it available worldwide, visit us online at www.trafford.com

ISBN: 978-1-4120-2984-1 (sc)

Print information available on the last page.

Trafford rev. 08/18/2022

Hi! My name is Mr. Happy Heart. I'm here to say that knowing about your heart is a great way to start your day.

Meet my pet Morgan. He is full of organs!

Not the kind that are played at church, but the organs that give you support.

In a body is where you will find them, coming in all different shapes and sizes.

The heart is an organ
your fist is its size.
Made out of muscle
are you surprised?

The heart is my favorite because it is full of love!

I never have to guess where it is coming from.

Please keep in mind that your heart is very special with many chores to do.

The most important chore is being a pump like the kind your great-great-grandmother would use!

"Lubb-dubb, lubb-dubb, lubb-dubb" your heart says all day and night long. A doctor can hear this sound when she moves her stethoscope all around.

One, two, three, four chambers make the heart whole.

Unless, of course, you are a frog, then three is all you really need.

One, two, three, four valves open and close just like doors.

Elephants, mice, monkeys and bears all have four valves...

just like those skunks over there!

One sure fire way to keep a healthy heart is to play all day...

and sleep all night.

The End.

Printed in the United States
by Baker & Taylor Publisher Services